Disney

DREAMS COLLECTION

THOMAS KINKADE
S T U D I O S

COLORING BOOK

Andrews McMeel
PUBLISHING®

Thomas
Kinkade

Mickey and Minnie–Sweetheart Cove

Snow White and the Seven Dwarfs

The Little Mermaid II

Beauty and the Beast Dancing in the Moonlight

Tinker Bell and Peter Pan Fly to Never Land

The Lion King

Aladdin

Pinocchio Wishes Upon a Star

Snow White Discovers the Cottage

Beauty and the Beast II

Dumbo

Winnie the Pooh II

Snow White Discovers the Cottage

The Little Mermaid

Beauty and the Beast II

Alice in Wonderland

Sleeping Beauty

The Princess and the Frog

The Little Mermaid II

The Jungle Book

Lady and the Tramp

Bambi's First Year

Beauty and the Beast Falling in Love

Fantasia

Lady and the Tramp

Alice in Wonderland

Winnie the Pooh II

The Jungle Book

Beauty and the Beast Falling in Love

Tangled

Sleeping Beauty

Pinocchio Wishes Upon a Star

Bambi's First Year

Mickey and Minnie–Sweetheart Bridge

The Little Mermaid

Snow White and the Seven Dwarfs

Fantasia

Cinderella Wishes Upon a Dream

Beauty and the Beast Falling in Love

Aladdin

Winnie the Pooh I

Dumbo

Sleeping Beauty

Peter Pan's Never Land

Pinocchio Wishes Upon a Star

Alice in Wonderland

Beauty and the Beast II

The Little Mermaid

The Lion King

Bambi's First Year

Lady and the Tramp

Beauty and the Beast Falling in Love

Cinderella Wishes Upon a Dream

The Little Mermaid

Alice in Wonderland

Snow White Discovers the Cottage

The Princess and the Frog

Tinker Bell and Peter Pan Fly to Never Land

Tangled

Winnie the Pooh I

Sleeping Beauty

Bambi's First Year

The Little Mermaid II